Rejecting Grasshopper Talk
From Grasshopper to Giant-Killer
Defeating Giants Daily!

Gerard Assey

Rejecting Grasshopper Talk
**From Grasshopper
to Giant-Killer**
Defeating Giants Daily!
By
Gerard Assey
© Copyright 2023 by Author

Published by:
Gerard Assey
19/18, Palli Arasan Street
Anna Nagar East
Chennai - 600 102

ISBN: 978-81-965807-3-5

*(Image by brgfx courtesy Freepik:
'https://www.freepik.com' Thank You)*

Table of Contents

Preface

In the vast annals of history, amidst the stories of courage and triumph, there exist narratives that illuminate the very essence of human potential—the tales that reveal the giant-killers among us. These stories transcend time and culture, serving as beacons of inspiration for generations. One such story, deeply rooted in the pages of the Bible, is that of Joshua and Caleb, two remarkable individuals who rejected the crippling "grasshopper talk" that permeated their ranks.

The biblical account of Moses sending twelve spies into the land of Canaan is more than just an ancient tale; it is a timeless lesson in faith, courage, and unwavering determination. Ten spies returned with reports of defeat and self-doubt, comparing themselves to grasshoppers in the presence of giants. However, Joshua and Caleb stood apart from the rest, refusing to succumb to the defeatist mindset. They declared, "We are well able to overcome the giants," and with faith as their guide, they did.

Rejecting Grasshopper Talk: From Grasshopper to Giant-Killer-*Defeating Giants Daily!* is a book born from this enduring story—a guide to conquering life's giants, irrespective of their form or magnitude. In its pages, you will embark on a journey that marries the wisdom of biblical narratives with the practicality of contemporary examples. You will explore the depths of the human psyche, uncovering the origins of self-doubt and the psychology behind it. You will learn the significance of diverse perspectives and the power of teamwork in decision-making. You will witness the crippling effects of negativity and the contagious nature of defeatism. You will be introduced to Joshua and Caleb, the giant-killers, and discover the qualities that set them apart—resilience, courage, and unwavering faith.

Throughout these chapters, you will find not just lessons but actionable plans and strategies for embracing a mindset of victory. You will learn how to reframe your perspective in the face of adversity, confront your fears with courage, and unleash the transformative power of faith. You will discover the critical role of action in turning belief into achievement and develop the resilience to navigate setbacks and challenges. Finally, you will be guided through the process of claiming your own "promised land"—the realization of your most cherished goals and dreams.

As you delve into these pages, remember that this book is not just about ancient stories or distant heroes; it is about you. It is about the giant-killer within you, waiting to be awakened and empowered. Whether you face personal challenges, professional aspirations, or dreams beyond measure, the principles within these chapters are your guiding stars.

This book is an invitation to reject grasshopper talk and, instead, embrace a mindset of faith, courage, and unwavering determination. It is a reminder that no matter the giants you encounter, you have the innate potential to conquer them.

May this journey be a source of inspiration, empowerment, and transformation in your life as you boldly claim your own promised land.

Embracing a Mindset of Faith, Courage, and Unwavering Determination

In the grand tapestry of human history, certain moments stand out as profound guides, illuminating the path to triumph over life's most daunting challenges. The story we are about to explore is one such moment, a testament to the enduring wisdom that empowers individuals to conquer even the most overwhelming odds. This chapter takes us deep into the heart of the biblical narrative, to a time when faith, courage, and an unwavering determination were the key to triumph.

This is a story of twelve individuals sent on a mission that went beyond the physical realm. It was a mission that tested not only their physical prowess but, more importantly, the strength of their minds and the depths of their faith. As they embarked on this mission to explore the promised land of Canaan, they carried with them the weight of a decision that would impact an entire nation.

The land they journeyed to was one of promise—a land flowing with milk and honey, filled with abundance and opportunity. Yet, within its bounteous embrace, it also cradled giants, formidable and intimidating. What these twelve explorers witnessed was not just a physical landscape but a reflection of their inner landscapes—a test of their mindset, their faith, and their courage.

Ten among them returned with a report that reflected not only what they saw but how they saw themselves. They described towering giants and themselves as insignificant grasshoppers in comparison. It was a narrative drenched in doubt and defeatism, a perspective that would go on to shape their destiny.

But within this narrative of despair and self-doubt, two individuals emerged as beacons of unwavering faith—Joshua and Caleb. They saw the same giants, encountered the same challenges, but their perspective was vastly different. To them, these giants were conquerable, and they were not mere grasshoppers. It was their mindset, grounded in faith and courage, that set them on a path to greatness.

This chapter marks the beginning of our journey—a journey into the heart of this timeless story, a story that transcends the bounds of time and culture. It is not merely a recounting of historical events but a living testament to the enduring lessons encapsulated in the narrative of Joshua, Caleb, and the ten spies.

Our exploration will delve deep into the psychology of mindset—the critical role it plays in our perception of challenges, our reactions to adversity, and our capacity to overcome giants. We will witness the diversity within the twelve explorers, a testament to the power of teamwork and collective influence.

Most importantly, we will dissect the qualities that set Joshua and Caleb apart as giant-killers. Their resilience, unyielding faith, and refusal to be defined by external circumstances hold invaluable lessons for all of us. We will understand that it is not just about conquering external giants but mastering the giants that reside within us—self-doubt, fear, and defeatism. As we progress, you will find practical guidance on how to cultivate a mindset grounded in faith, courage, and unwavering determination. You will learn how to reframe your perspective, conquer fear, and navigate setbacks on your path to victory. But at the heart of it all, you will come to realize the profound importance of the right mindset—a mindset that can transform giants into stepping stones.

This chapter is your gateway to a journey of self-discovery and empowerment. It's an invitation to embrace a mindset that will enable you to boldly face the giants in your life, whether they be personal challenges, societal obstacles, or the weight of self-doubt. The lessons contained within these pages are timeless, and they are your guide to unlocking your limitless potential.

As we embark on this journey together, may you find inspiration, wisdom, and guidance. May you discover, within the recesses of your being, the giant-killer you were meant to be—a person of faith, courage, and unwavering determination.

Importance of Avoiding Grasshopper Talk and Instead Focusing on the Power of GOD to Overcome Giants

Avoiding "grasshopper talk" and instead concentrating on the power of God to help us overcome our giants is essential for several reasons, and here are some reasons along with examples:

1. **Fostering Faith and Belief:** Embracing the power of God reinforces our faith and belief in divine assistance. When we trust in God's ability to guide and support us, we are more likely to take bold steps towards our goals. For instance, Joshua and Caleb's unshakable faith in God's promise to give them the land of Canaan empowered them to face the giants with courage.

2. **Overcoming Self-Doubt:** "Grasshopper talk" often stems from self-doubt and insecurity. When we focus on God's power, we can overcome our insecurities and recognize our worth and potential. An example from the Bible is Gideon, who initially doubted his ability to lead the Israelites but found strength and confidence through God's assurance (Judges 6).

3. **Inspiration and Motivation:** Believing in God's power can be a powerful source of inspiration and motivation. When we reflect on stories like David's triumph over Goliath, we are motivated to face our own giants with determination and courage.

4. **Resilience in Adversity:** Trusting in God's power helps us endure and persevere through adversity. Job, in the Bible, is a prime example of unwavering faith and resilience in the face of immense suffering and loss.

5. **Guidance and Direction:** When we acknowledge God's guidance, we are more likely to seek His wisdom and direction in our decision-making. Like Solomon, who asked God for wisdom to lead his people (1 Kings 3), we can seek divine guidance in our choices.

6. **Maintaining Positivity:** Focusing on God's power helps us maintain a positive outlook, even in challenging circumstances. Joseph, despite facing betrayal and imprisonment, held onto his faith and positivity, ultimately rising to a position of power and influence (Genesis 39-41).

7. **Unity and Community:** Believing in God's power can foster unity within communities. When the Israelites trusted in God during their exodus from Egypt, it strengthened their sense of community and purpose, enabling them to overcome numerous challenges together.

8. **Coping with Fear:** Trusting in God's power can help us cope with fear and anxiety. As Daniel did in the lion's den (Daniel 6) and as Jesus demonstrated in the Garden of Gethsemane (Matthew 26), we can find strength and peace in God's presence during times of fear.

9. **Transforming Challenges into Opportunities:** Instead of seeing challenges as insurmountable obstacles, we can view

them as opportunities for God to work in our lives. The Apostle Paul, who faced numerous hardships, found that God's grace was sufficient to turn his weaknesses into strengths (2 Corinthians 12).

10. **Hope and Endurance:** Belief in God's power provides hope and endurance during long and difficult journeys. Just as the Israelites endured forty years in the wilderness, we can endure and persevere with the hope of reaching our own promised lands.

In summary, avoiding "grasshopper talk" and placing our trust in God's power offers us faith, resilience, motivation, guidance, unity, and the ability to cope with fear. It transforms our challenges into opportunities and provides us with hope and endurance on our life's journey, enabling us to overcome our giants with unwavering determination.

The Grasshopper Mentality

As we embark on our journey to reject the crippling "grasshopper mentality," we begin by delving deep into the origins of this mindset that so often hinders our progress. This chapter explores the intricate web of thoughts, emotions, and beliefs that cause individuals to perceive themselves as powerless and insignificant when confronted by life's formidable giants. We'll not only examine the psychology behind such thinking but also dissect its detrimental impact on personal growth and achievement.

Lesson 1: Recognizing the Grasshopper Mentality

Bible Verse: Numbers 13:32-33
"And they brought up an evil report of the land which they had searched unto the children of Israel, saying... And there we saw the giants... and we were in our own sight as grasshoppers, and so we were in their sight."

Biblical Example: The Ten Spies

The biblical account of the ten spies serves as a poignant illustration of the grasshopper mentality. When faced with the opportunity to enter the promised land of Canaan, these men allowed fear and self-doubt to shape their perception. They saw themselves as powerless grasshoppers in the presence of giants, and this perception had a profound impact on their actions and decisions.

Action Plan: Overcoming the Grasshopper Mentality

1. **Self-awareness:** The first step towards overcoming the grasshopper mentality is to recognize when it takes hold. Pay close attention to your thoughts and feelings when facing challenges. Are you underestimating your abilities or dwelling on your perceived inadequacies?

2. **Challenge limiting beliefs:** Examine the beliefs that contribute to your grasshopper mentality. Are these beliefs based on facts or assumptions? Challenge them with evidence of your past successes and capabilities.

3. **Positive affirmations:** Practice positive self-talk. Replace self-deprecating thoughts with affirmations that reinforce your self-worth and capabilities. Remind yourself of your strengths and past achievements.

4. **Seek inspiration:** Surround yourself with stories of individuals who have overcome immense challenges. Read about Joshua and Caleb, who refused to embrace the grasshopper mentality. Draw inspiration from their unwavering faith.

5. **Set achievable goals:** Break down your goals into smaller, manageable steps. Achieving these smaller victories will boost your confidence and help you build a more positive self-image.

6. **Embrace failure as a learning opportunity:** Understand that setbacks are a part of life. Instead of seeing them as confirmation of your limitations, view them as valuable learning experiences that contribute to your growth.

7. **Cultivate a growth mindset:** Adopt the belief that your abilities and intelligence can be

developed through dedication and hard work. A growth mindset encourages resilience and perseverance.

8. **Seek support:** Don't hesitate to seek guidance and support from friends, family, or a mentor. They can provide valuable perspective and encouragement during challenging times.

Discussion Questions to Encourage Self-reflection and Group Discussions

These discussion questions can serve as conversation starters for group study, book clubs, or personal reflection, helping you explore the book's themes and apply its principles to your own lives.

- ✓ What are some common situations in your life where you've experienced a "grasshopper mentality"? How did it affect your actions and decisions?
- ✓ Reflect on a time when you overcame self-doubt and embraced a mindset of faith and courage. What strategies or beliefs helped you do this?
- ✓ How can understanding the origins of the grasshopper mentality empower you to overcome it in the future?

By diligently applying these strategies and lessons, you can begin to break free from the grip of the grasshopper mentality. In doing so, you'll take your first step toward a mindset of courage and self-belief, setting the stage for the journey to conquer your own giants. Remember, the battle against the grasshopper mentality is not won overnight, but with persistence and determination, you can rewrite the narrative of your life and embrace your true potential.

The Twelve Spies

In this chapter, we embark on a journey to acquaint ourselves with the twelve individuals chosen by Moses to explore the land of Canaan. Each of these spies brings a unique background, set of beliefs, and mindset to the table. As we delve into their diverse perspectives, we will gain valuable insights into the importance of teamwork, diversity in decision-making, and the profound influence of collective thinking on our perceptions and choices.

Lesson 2: The Power of Diversity and Teamwork

Bible Verse: Numbers 13:2
"Send thou men, that they may search the land of Canaan, which I give unto the children of Israel: of every tribe of their fathers shall ye send a man, every one a ruler among them."

Biblical Example: The Twelve Spies

The selection of twelve spies, one from each tribe, exemplifies the concept of diversity and teamwork. These men came from various backgrounds and held different beliefs and mindsets. This diversity could have been a tremendous asset, providing a range of perspectives and insights.

Action Plan: Embracing Diversity and Teamwork

1. **Recognize the value of diversity:** Acknowledge that diversity in perspectives and backgrounds can enrich decision-making processes. Different viewpoints can lead to more well-rounded and informed choices.

2. **Promote open communication:** Encourage open and respectful dialogue among team members. Create an environment where individuals feel comfortable sharing their ideas and concerns.
3. **Seek diverse input:** Actively seek out input from individuals with different backgrounds and experiences when making important decisions. Avoid groupthink by welcoming dissenting opinions.
4. **Build diverse teams:** When forming teams for projects or tasks, consider assembling groups with a mix of skills, experiences, and perspectives. This diversity can lead to creative solutions.
5. **Practice active listening:** Take the time to truly listen to others' viewpoints. Show empathy and respect for their perspectives, even if they differ from your own.
6. **Collaborate effectively:** Foster a culture of collaboration and cooperation. Encourage team members to work together toward common goals and objectives.
7. **Value individual strengths:** Recognize and leverage the unique strengths and talents that each team member brings to the table. This can lead to more effective problem-solving and decision-making.
8. **Reflect on collective decisions:** After making a decision as a team, take time to evaluate its outcomes and learn from the process. Use this feedback to improve future decision-making.

Discussion Questions to Encourage Self-reflection and Group Discussions

These discussion questions can serve as conversation starters for group study, book clubs, or personal reflection, helping you explore the book's themes and apply its principles to your own lives.

- ✓ Consider the diversity among the twelve spies in the Bible story. How can diverse perspectives enhance decision-making in your personal and professional life?
- ✓ Share an experience when you were part of a team or group with diverse viewpoints. How did the collective influence of the group shape the outcome?
- ✓ How can you apply the lessons from the twelve spies' story to foster better teamwork and decision-making in your own life?

By embracing the lessons of diversity and teamwork demonstrated by the twelve spies, you can enhance your own decision-making processes and perspectives. Remember that while diversity may bring about differing viewpoints, it also has the potential to lead to more robust, well-rounded choices. Just as the twelve spies were chosen to explore the land of Canaan as a diverse group, your willingness to embrace diversity and teamwork can help you navigate the challenging landscapes of life and overcome the giants that stand in your way.

The Defeatist Report

We will now turn our attention to the pivotal moment when the ten spies returned from their mission in Canaan bearing a report that would reverberate through history. We will meticulously analyze this report, dissecting not only the words but also the imagery it conveyed. More importantly, we will explore the profound and crippling effect it had on the faith and morale of the Israelite community. This chapter serves as a cautionary tale, illustrating how negativity can spread like wildfire, paralyzing a community and hindering progress.

Lesson 3: The Destructive Power of Negativity
Bible Verse: Numbers 13:32-33
"And they brought up an evil report of the land which they had searched unto the children of Israel, saying... And there we saw the giants... and we were in our own sight as grasshoppers, and so we were in their sight."

Biblical Example: The Ten Spies' Report
The report delivered by the ten spies is a stark example of the destructive power of negativity. Their words painted a grim picture of their own capabilities and the challenges they faced. The imagery of feeling like grasshoppers in the presence of giants not only reflected their own self-doubt but also projected fear onto the entire community.

Action Plan: Combating Negativity
1. **Self-awareness:** Be mindful of your own negative thoughts and words. Recognize

when you are engaging in defeatist talk or spreading negativity.

2. **Challenge negative narratives:** When faced with challenges or setbacks, question the narratives you create. Are you catastrophizing the situation? Are there alternative, more positive perspectives to consider?

3. **Encourage positive communication:** Foster an environment where positive and constructive communication is encouraged. Lead by example by using uplifting language and focusing on solutions rather than problems.

4. **Limit exposure to negativity:** Be selective about the media and information you consume. Excessive exposure to negative news or pessimistic individuals can influence your own mindset.

5. **Surround yourself with positivity:** Build a network of supportive and optimistic friends and mentors. Their positivity can be contagious and uplifting.

6. **Practice gratitude:** Regularly reflect on the things you are grateful for in your life. This can help shift your focus away from negativity and toward appreciation.

7. **Take positive action:** Instead of dwelling on problems, channel your energy into finding solutions and taking proactive steps. Action can counteract the paralyzing effects of negativity.

8. **Seek professional help:** If negativity and pessimism are deeply ingrained, consider seeking the guidance of a therapist or

counselor who can provide strategies for changing thought patterns.

Discussion Questions to Encourage Self-reflection and Group Discussions

These discussion questions can serve as conversation starters for group study, book clubs, or personal reflection, helping you explore the book's themes and apply its principles to your own lives.

- ✓ Think about a time when negative words or thoughts had a crippling effect on your faith or morale. What did you learn from that experience?
- ✓ How can you guard against the spread of defeatism in your community or workplace, and instead, promote a positive and hopeful atmosphere?
- ✓ Share an example of a person, historical figure, or leader who refused to accept a defeatist report and went on to achieve remarkable success. What inspired their resilience?

By taking deliberate steps to combat negativity in your own life and within your community, you can prevent the spread of defeatist talk and its paralyzing effects. Remember that your words and attitudes have the power to influence those around you, and by choosing positivity and resilience, you can inspire others to do the same. Just as the ten spies' report had a far-reaching impact, your commitment to fostering a positive and hopeful mindset can contribute to your personal growth and success in overcoming life's giants.

Joshua and Caleb: The Giant-Killers

In this chapter, we turn our attention to two extraordinary individuals who stood as beacons of hope amidst the prevailing defeatism—the incomparable Joshua and Caleb. These two outliers defied the pervasive grasshopper talk that had seized the hearts and minds of their peers. As we delve into their stories, we will uncover the unique qualities, unwavering mindset, and steadfast faith that set them apart as giant-killers. This chapter is a testament to the transformative power of resilience, courage, and faith in the pursuit of success.

Lesson 4: The Triumph of Unwavering Faith

Bible Verse: Numbers 14:24
"But my servant Caleb, because he had another spirit with him, and hath followed me fully, him will I bring into the land whereinto he went, and his seed shall possess it."

Biblical Example: Joshua and Caleb

Joshua and Caleb's unwavering faith in the face of overwhelming adversity is a shining example for all generations. While the majority succumbed to fear and doubt, these two men remained resolute in their belief that they could conquer the giants and inherit the Promised Land. Their faith was not blind; it was rooted in their trust in the divine promise and their own abilities.

Action Plan: Cultivating Unwavering Faith

1. **Clarify your purpose:** Understand your life's purpose and align your goals with it. A clear

sense of purpose can fuel your faith and determination.

2. **Strengthen your belief system:** Cultivate a strong belief system that encompasses your values, principles, and core convictions. These beliefs will serve as a foundation for your faith.

3. **Draw inspiration from role models:** Study the lives of individuals who have demonstrated unwavering faith and resilience. Learn from their experiences and apply their principles to your own journey.

4. **Surround yourself with positivity:** Engage with positive and supportive individuals who can nurture your faith and encourage your pursuit of goals.

5. **Maintain a resilient mindset:** Develop mental resilience by viewing setbacks as opportunities for growth rather than insurmountable obstacles. Embrace challenges as stepping stones toward success.

6. **Seek guidance through prayer or meditation:** Many find solace and strength in prayer or meditation. These practices can help you connect with your inner beliefs and find inspiration.

7. **Set achievable milestones:** Break your larger goals into smaller, manageable milestones. Each accomplishment will reinforce your faith and confidence.

8. **Celebrate your successes:** Acknowledge and celebrate your achievements, no matter how small they may seem. This positive

reinforcement can bolster your faith in your abilities.

Discussion Questions to Encourage Self-reflection and Group Discussions

These discussion questions can serve as conversation starters for group study, book clubs, or personal reflection, helping you explore the book's themes and apply its principles to your own lives.

- ✓ Identify the unique qualities and mindset that set Joshua and Caleb apart as giant-killers. Which of these qualities do you possess, and which would you like to develop further?
- ✓ Reflect on a time when you demonstrated resilience and unwavering faith in the face of adversity. What was the outcome, and what kept you going?
- ✓ How can you apply the lessons from Joshua and Caleb's story to your own life to become a giant-killer in your challenges and pursuits?

By cultivating unwavering faith, you can develop the resilience and courage needed to confront and conquer the giants in your life. Remember that faith is not blind optimism; it is a deep-seated belief in your capabilities, guided by a clear sense of purpose. Joshua and Caleb serve as living proof that faith, when combined with action, can lead to the fulfillment of even the most audacious dreams. Their stories inspire us to cultivate a spirit of unwavering faith as we navigate the challenges and giants on our own paths to success.

Reframing Your Perspective

One of the most important lessons here is the profound art of reframing your perspective- a skill that becomes particularly crucial when facing adversity. We will explore practical techniques and strategies that can help you shift from a grasshopper mentality, characterized by self-doubt and defeatism, to a giant-killer mindset filled with confidence and determination. Real-life examples of individuals who have conquered seemingly insurmountable challenges will serve as beacons of inspiration and guidance.

Lesson 5: The Power of Perspective Transformation

Bible Verse: Romans 12:2
"Do not conform to the pattern of this world, but be transformed by the renewing of your mind. Then you will be able to test and approve what God's will is— his good, pleasing and perfect will."

Biblical Example: The Transformation of Joshua and Caleb

Joshua and Caleb's transformation from ordinary spies to giant-killers is a testament to the power of perspective transformation. When they first set foot in Canaan, they faced the same daunting giants as their peers. However, they chose to see the situation differently. Instead of viewing themselves as grasshoppers, they recognized their own strength and believed in their ability to overcome the challenges ahead.

Action Plan: Reframing Your Perspective
1. **Identify negative thought patterns:** Start by recognizing and acknowledging the negative thought patterns that hold you back. Are you prone to self-doubt, catastrophizing, or focusing on limitations?
2. **Challenge your thoughts:** When negative thoughts arise, challenge them. Ask yourself if they are based on facts or assumptions. Are there alternative, more positive ways to view the situation?
3. **Practice gratitude:** Regularly reflect on the things you are grateful for in your life. Shifting your focus to the positive aspects can help reframe your perspective.
4. **Seek diverse input:** When facing challenges, seek input from others with different perspectives. They may offer insights that you hadn't considered, opening up new possibilities.
5. **Visualize success:** Create a mental image of yourself successfully overcoming challenges. Visualization can help you build confidence and belief in your abilities.
6. **Use affirmations:** Develop a set of positive affirmations that reinforce your self-worth and capabilities. Repeat them daily to reprogram your subconscious mind.
7. **Learn from adversity:** Instead of viewing setbacks as failures, see them as opportunities for growth. What lessons can you glean from adversity? How can it make you stronger?
8. **Surround yourself with positivity:** Engage with individuals who inspire and uplift you.

Their positivity can influence your own perspective.

Discussion Questions to Encourage Self-reflection and Group Discussions

These discussion questions can serve as conversation starters for group study, book clubs, or personal reflection, helping you explore the book's themes and apply its principles to your own lives.

- ✓ Share an experience when you successfully reframed your perspective to view a challenge as an opportunity. How did this shift in mindset affect your approach and outcomes?
- ✓ Explore the concept of "seeing giants as stepping stones." What giants in your life could potentially become stepping stones to your growth and success?
- ✓ What practical techniques or strategies can you use to shift from a grasshopper mentality to a giant-killer mindset in your daily life?

By diligently applying these strategies and lessons, you can gradually reframe your perspective in the face of adversity. Transformation may not happen overnight, but as you consistently practice these techniques, you will develop the ability to view challenges as opportunities and replace self-doubt with self-assuredness. Real-life examples of individuals who have achieved this transformation will provide you with inspiration and serve as living proof that a giant-killer mindset is within your reach. As you continue on your journey, remember that the power to reshape your perspective lies within you, waiting to be unlocked and harnessed for your own success and fulfillment.

Overcoming Fear

In this chapter, we confront one of the most formidable adversaries of the human spirit: fear. Fear often lies at the heart of the grasshopper mentality, paralyzing individuals and preventing them from realizing their full potential. We will dive deep into the nature of fear, gaining insights into its origin and understanding its impact on our lives. Drawing from both biblical and contemporary stories, we will explore the tools and strategies for building confidence and courage even in the face of the most daunting circumstances.

Lesson 6: Conquering Fear and Building Courage
Bible Verse: 2 Timothy 1:7
"For God hath not given us the spirit of fear; but of power, and of love, and of a sound mind."

Biblical Example: David and Goliath
The story of David and Goliath is an iconic biblical example of conquering fear. David, a young shepherd, faced the giant warrior Goliath in a battle that seemed hopelessly one-sided. While others cowered in fear, David stood tall, armed with faith and courage. His unwavering belief in God's power overcame his fear, leading to victory.

Action Plan: Conquering Fear and Cultivating Courage
1. **Identify your fears:** Begin by recognizing and acknowledging your fears. What are you afraid of? Understanding your fears is the first step to conquering them.

2. **Examine the source of fear:** Delve into the root causes of your fears. Are they based on past experiences, limiting beliefs, or irrational anxieties? Understanding the source can help you address them more effectively.
3. **Challenge irrational beliefs:** When fear is based on irrational beliefs, challenge them with rational thinking. Seek evidence that contradicts your fears and supports your ability to overcome challenges.
4. **Practice mindfulness:** Mindfulness meditation can help you become more aware of your thoughts and emotions. This awareness can provide you with greater control over your fear responses.
5. **Visualization:** Visualize yourself successfully facing and conquering your fears. This mental rehearsal can build confidence and reduce anxiety.
6. **Take gradual steps:** Gradual exposure to your fears can desensitize you to them over time. Start with small steps and gradually increase your level of exposure.
7. **Seek support:** Don't hesitate to seek support from friends, family, or a therapist. Talking about your fears can provide emotional relief and new perspectives.
8. **Develop a mantra:** Create a personal mantra or affirmation that reinforces your courage and strength. Repeat it during challenging moments to boost your confidence.
9. **Embrace failure as a teacher:** Understand that failure is a natural part of life. Instead of fearing it, view it as an opportunity for growth and learning.

10. **Practice self-compassion:** Be kind to yourself when facing fears. Avoid self-criticism, and treat yourself with the same compassion you would offer to a friend in a similar situation.

Discussion Questions to Encourage Self-reflection and Group Discussions

These discussion questions can serve as conversation starters for group study, book clubs, or personal reflection, helping you explore the book's themes and apply its principles to your own lives.

- ✓ Reflect on the role of fear in your life. How has fear held you back from pursuing your goals or facing challenges head-on?
- ✓ Share an example of a person or character from history or literature who conquered their fears with courage. What qualities did they exhibit, and how can you apply them?
- ✓ What steps can you take to conquer fear and build confidence and courage in daunting circumstances?

By diligently applying these strategies and lessons, you can confront and conquer fear, transforming it from a paralyzing force into a catalyst for personal growth and courage. The story of David and Goliath teaches us that courage is not the absence of fear but the willingness to act in spite of it. As you cultivate this courage within yourself, you'll find the strength to face life's giants with determination, knowing that you possess the power to overcome fear and achieve your dreams.

The Power of Faith

We will now also look at the importance of another aspect- that of faith, by drawing inspiration from the unwavering belief of Joshua and Caleb. We will uncover the transformative power of faith through their remarkable journey, discovering how it can move mountains and lead to victorious outcomes. Readers will gain invaluable insights into nurturing and strengthening their own faith, even in the face of adversity.

Lesson 7: Unleashing the Transformative Power of Faith

Bible Verse: Hebrews 11:1
"Now faith is the substance of things hoped for, the evidence of things not seen."

Biblical Example: Joshua and Caleb's Faith

Joshua and Caleb's faith was unshakable, even when faced with seemingly insurmountable challenges. They believed in God's promise to give them the land of Canaan, and this faith propelled them forward. Their unwavering trust in the divine plan not only sustained them but also led them to victory.

Action Plan: Nurturing and Strengthening Your Faith

1. **Cultivate a deep sense of purpose:** Faith is often rooted in a sense of purpose. Clarify your life's purpose and align your actions with it to strengthen your faith.

2. **Study and reflection:** Spend time studying and reflecting on your beliefs. Seek to understand the foundations of your faith and the values that guide your life.
3. **Prayer and meditation:** Engage in regular prayer or meditation to deepen your connection with your faith and seek guidance in times of doubt or adversity.
4. **Surround yourself with faith-filled influences:** Associate with individuals who share your faith and can provide support and encouragement during challenging times.
5. **Practice gratitude:** Express gratitude for the blessings in your life. Recognizing and appreciating what you have can strengthen your faith in a higher power.
6. **Engage in acts of service:** Serving others can deepen your faith and sense of purpose. It connects you to a larger, meaningful mission.
7. **Face fear with faith:** When confronted with fear or doubt, turn to your faith for solace and strength. Remind yourself of past experiences where faith carried you through.
8. **Keep a faith journal:** Maintain a journal where you record your thoughts, prayers, and moments of inspiration. Reflecting on your journey can fortify your faith.
9. **Seek wisdom:** Explore religious texts, books, and teachings that align with your faith. They can provide valuable insights and guidance.
10. **Surround yourself with symbols of faith:** Incorporate symbols or reminders of your faith into your daily life. These visual cues can serve as powerful reminders of your beliefs.

Discussion Questions to Encourage Self-reflection and Group Discussions

These discussion questions can serve as conversation starters for group study, book clubs, or personal reflection, helping you explore the book's themes and apply its principles to your own lives.

- ✓ Describe a situation in your life where faith played a significant role in your success or perseverance. How did your faith impact your actions and decisions?
- ✓ Consider the phrase "faith can move mountains." What "mountains" in your life do you believe faith can help you overcome?
- ✓ What daily practices or rituals can you implement to nurture and strengthen your faith in the face of adversity?

By actively nurturing and strengthening your faith, you can tap into the transformative power that guided Joshua and Caleb on their journey. Remember that faith is not a passive state but an active force that propels you forward, even when facing giants. As you cultivate your faith, you'll find the strength and resilience to overcome adversity and achieve victory in your own life. Just as Joshua and Caleb's faith led them to the promised land, your unwavering belief can lead you to the fulfillment of your own dreams and aspirations.

Taking Action

In this chapter, we explore the pivotal role that action plays in the journey from belief to achievement. Action is the bridge that transforms our beliefs into tangible results, and it is a crucial component in the process of overcoming life's giants. We will delve into the significance of taking proactive steps, offering practical advice and real-life examples of individuals who turned their beliefs into remarkable accomplishments.

Lesson 8: The Power of Action

Bible Verse: James 2:17
"In the same way, faith by itself, if it is not accompanied by action, is dead."

Biblical Example: The Israelites' Journey to Canaan

The Israelites' journey from Egypt to Canaan is a profound biblical example of the power of action. Their faith in God's promise to lead them to the promised land was demonstrated through their physical actions—crossing the Red Sea, facing challenges in the wilderness, and ultimately entering Canaan. Their belief was translated into action, leading to the fulfillment of God's promise.

Action Plan: Turning Belief into Achievement

1. **Set clear, achievable goals:** Define specific, measurable, and time-bound goals that align with your beliefs and aspirations. This clarity provides direction and motivation.

2. **Break goals into actionable steps:** Divide larger goals into smaller, manageable tasks. This prevents overwhelm and allows for incremental progress.
3. **Create a plan:** Develop a detailed plan outlining the actions required to achieve your goals. Consider potential obstacles and devise strategies to overcome them.
4. **Take the first step:** Overcoming inertia is often the most challenging part. Commit to taking the first step, no matter how small it may be.
5. **Stay consistent:** Consistency is key to making progress. Establish daily or weekly routines that align with your goals and beliefs.
6. **Embrace failure as part of the process:** Understand that setbacks and failures are natural on the path to achievement. Use them as learning opportunities and motivation to persist.
7. **Seek guidance and mentorship:** Learn from individuals who have achieved what you aspire to. Seek out mentors or role models who can offer guidance and support.
8. **Celebrate milestones:** Acknowledge and celebrate your achievements along the way. These celebrations provide motivation and reinforce your belief in your capabilities.
9. **Adapt and refine your approach:** Be flexible in your actions. If something isn't working, don't be afraid to adjust your strategy and try a different approach.
10. **Stay accountable:** Share your goals and progress with a trusted friend or mentor who can hold you accountable for your actions.

Discussion Questions to Encourage Self-reflection and Group Discussions

These discussion questions can serve as conversation starters for group study, book clubs, or personal reflection, helping you explore the book's themes and apply its principles to your own lives.

- ✓ Think about a time when you turned your beliefs into tangible results through action. What motivated you to take that action, and what were the outcomes?
- ✓ How can you bridge the gap between belief and achievement in your current goals and aspirations?
- ✓ Share a personal or historical example of someone who took decisive action to overcome giants in their life. What can you learn from their experience?

Taking action is the bridge that transforms belief into achievement. It is through the tangible steps we take that we make progress and ultimately conquer life's giants. The biblical journey of the Israelites reminds us that faith alone is not enough; it must be accompanied by action. By following the action plan and strategies outlined in this chapter, you can harness the power of action to propel yourself toward the fulfillment of your dreams and aspirations. Just as the Israelites entered the promised land through their actions, you too can conquer your own giants and claim your own promised land of success and fulfillment.

Navigating Setbacks

As we move forward, in this chapter, we delve into a universal truth: even giant-killers encounter setbacks on their path to victory. We explore how Joshua and Caleb, despite their unwavering faith and determination, faced disappointments and challenges during their journey to conquer Canaan. Through their experiences, readers will gain profound insights into the qualities of resilience and perseverance, which are essential for overcoming life's obstacles.

Lesson 9: Embracing Resilience and Perseverance

Bible Verse: Romans 5:3-4
"Not only so, but we also glory in our sufferings because we know that suffering produces perseverance; perseverance, character; and character, hope."

Biblical Example: Joshua and Caleb's Setbacks

Joshua and Caleb, although filled with faith and determination, encountered setbacks on their journey to Canaan. Their initial report to Moses and the Israelites fell on deaf ears, leading to forty years of wandering in the wilderness. During this time, they faced numerous challenges and disappointments, but they never wavered in their belief that they would eventually reach the promised land.

Action Plan: Building Resilience and Perseverance

Accept setbacks as part of the journey: Understand that setbacks are a natural part of any endeavor. Accept them as opportunities for growth and learning.

Maintain a growth mindset: Embrace a mindset that views setbacks as opportunities to develop resilience and character. Focus on what you can learn from each setback.

Seek support: Lean on the support of friends, family, or mentors during challenging times. They can offer guidance, perspective, and encouragement.

Adapt and adjust: When faced with setbacks, be willing to adapt and adjust your approach. Consider alternative strategies and solutions.

Stay committed to your goals: Revisit your goals and remind yourself why they are important to you. This renewed commitment can rekindle your determination.

Celebrate small victories: Acknowledge and celebrate even the smallest victories and progress made in the face of setbacks. These celebrations can provide motivation.

Learn from failure: View failure as a valuable teacher. Reflect on what went wrong and how you can apply these lessons in future endeavors.

Maintain perspective: Keep the bigger picture in mind. While setbacks may be discouraging in the short term, they do not define your overall journey.

Practice self-compassion: Be kind to yourself during setbacks. Avoid self-blame and self-criticism, and treat yourself with the same compassion you would offer to a friend.

Visualize success: Continue to visualize yourself achieving your goals, even in the face of setbacks. This mental rehearsal can maintain your motivation.

Discussion Questions to Encourage Self-reflection and Group Discussions

These discussion questions can serve as conversation starters for group study, book clubs, or personal reflection, helping you explore the book's themes and apply its principles to your own lives.

- ✓ Reflect on a setback or disappointment you've faced. How did you respond to it, and what did you learn from the experience?
- ✓ Consider the concept of resilience in the face of setbacks. What strategies or coping mechanisms have helped you bounce back from challenges?
- ✓ How can setbacks be viewed as opportunities for growth and development in your life?

By embracing setbacks with resilience and perseverance, you can navigate the challenges on your journey to conquer life's giants. Remember that setbacks are not roadblocks but stepping stones, shaping your character and building your resolve. Joshua and Caleb's unwavering faith and persistence eventually led them to the promised land. Similarly, your resilience and perseverance will carry you through, enabling you to triumph over adversity and achieve your own remarkable victories.

Claiming Your Promised Land

In this final chapter, we embark on a journey that culminates in the process of claiming your own "promised land." This metaphor symbolizes the realization of your most cherished goals, dreams, and aspirations. Drawing inspiration from the timeless biblical narrative, we offer a roadmap to victory, guiding you toward the fulfillment of your deepest desires.

Lesson 10: The Journey to Claiming Your Promised Land

Bible Verse: Joshua 1:9
"Have I not commanded you? Be strong and courageous. Do not be afraid; do not be discouraged, for the Lord your God will be with you wherever you go."

Biblical Example: The Israelites' Entry into Canaan

The Israelites' long and arduous journey through the wilderness, guided by their faith and led by Joshua, ultimately led them to the fulfillment of God's promise—the land of Canaan. Despite challenges, setbacks, and uncertainty, they claimed their promised land through unwavering faith, perseverance, and a steadfast commitment to their goal.

Action Plan: Claiming Your Promised Land

1. **Define your "promised land":** Clearly identify your goals, dreams, and aspirations.

What does your promised land look like? What do you aim to achieve?

2. **Create a vision:** Visualize your desired outcomes. Create a vivid mental image of what it will be like to achieve your goals. This vision will serve as your guiding star.

3. **Develop a strategic plan:** Outline the specific steps and actions required to reach your goals. Break them down into manageable tasks and prioritize them.

4. **Stay committed to your vision:** Revisit your vision regularly to remind yourself of the ultimate destination. Let it fuel your determination and enthusiasm.

5. **Build a support network:** Surround yourself with individuals who believe in your vision and can provide encouragement, guidance, and accountability.

6. **Embrace challenges as opportunities:** View challenges and setbacks as stepping stones on your journey. They offer valuable lessons and opportunities for growth.

7. **Practice perseverance:** Stay the course even when the path gets tough. Keep your determination alive and your faith unwavering.

8. **Celebrate achievements:** Acknowledge and celebrate each milestone and accomplishment along the way. This positive reinforcement fuels motivation.

9. **Seek continuous improvement:** Be open to learning and adaptation. As you progress, continually refine your approach to optimize your chances of success.

10. **Maintain gratitude:** Throughout your journey, remain grateful for the opportunities, support,

and progress you experience. Gratitude keeps your heart open to abundance.

11. **Stay resilient:** Cultivate resilience by bouncing back from setbacks and maintaining your determination. Resilience will sustain you through adversity.
12. **Pay it forward:** Share your journey and lessons learned with others. Inspire and support those who aspire to claim their own promised lands.

Discussion Questions to Encourage Self-reflection and Group Discussions

These discussion questions can serve as conversation starters for group study, book clubs, or personal reflection, helping you explore the book's themes and apply its principles to your own lives.

- ✓ Identify your personal "promised land" or goals and aspirations. What steps can you take to actively work toward claiming them?
- ✓ Reflect on the importance of having a vision and purpose in life. How can defining your vision help you stay motivated and focused?
- ✓ Share an example of someone who successfully claimed their "promised land." What qualities and strategies did they employ, and how can you apply them to your own journey?

Claiming your promised land is not a solitary endeavor; it is a testament to the power of faith, determination, and action. Just as the Israelites conquered Canaan through their unwavering belief and tenacity, you too can achieve your goals and fulfill your dreams. Your journey may be challenging, but it is through these challenges that you will grow and evolve into the person capable of claiming your own promised land. As you take the final steps on your journey, remember that you have the strength and guidance to realize your deepest desires and achieve remarkable victories in life.

The Power of Community

In the journey of rejecting grasshopper talk and embracing a giant-killer mindset, one of the most influential factors is the power of community. Throughout history, individuals who have achieved greatness often did so with the support, encouragement, and accountability of a community of like-minded individuals. This chapter explores the profound impact that community can have on your ability to conquer giants and thrive in faith.

Lesson 11: The Strength of Unity
"Two are better than one because they have a good return for their labor: If either of them falls down, one can help the other up." - Ecclesiastes 4:9-10
Biblical Examples/Characters Demonstrating the Lesson:
- ✓ The early Christian community in Acts 2, who shared everything and supported each other in times of need.
- ✓ Moses, who leaned on the support of Aaron and Hur during the battle against the Amalekites (Exodus 17:10-13).

Action Plan and Strategies to Develop This Further:
- ✓ Reflect on your current support system. Who are the individuals who encourage and uplift you in your faith journey? How can you strengthen these relationships?
- ✓ Consider joining or forming a small group, Bible study, or support network within your

church or community to foster a sense of unity and shared faith.
- ✓ Actively seek opportunities to support and pray for others in your community. Sometimes, helping someone else overcome their giants can empower you to do the same.

Lesson 2: Accountability and Growth

"As iron sharpens iron, so one person sharpens another." - Proverbs 27:17

Biblical Examples/Characters Demonstrating the Lesson:

- ✓ Paul and Timothy, who had a mentorship and accountability relationship (2 Timothy 2:2).
- ✓ David and Jonathan, whose friendship and mutual support were instrumental in their lives (1 Samuel 18:1-4).

Action Plan and Strategies to Develop This Further:

- ✓ Seek out a mentor or spiritual advisor who can provide guidance and hold you accountable in your faith journey.
- ✓ Consider setting regular goals and sharing them with an accountability partner. This will help you stay focused on rejecting grasshopper talk and pursuing giant-killer faith.
- ✓ Be open to providing accountability and support to others in your community. Your encouragement can help them reject defeatist mindsets as well.

Lesson 3: Encouragement and Prayer

"Therefore encourage one another and build each other up." - 1 Thessalonians 5:11

Biblical Examples/Characters Demonstrating the Lesson:
- ✓ Barnabas, whose name means "Son of Encouragement," played a pivotal role in supporting Paul and Mark in their ministry (Acts 4:36; Acts 15:36-41).
- ✓ The Apostle Paul frequently mentioned the importance of prayer and encouragement in his letters to various Christian communities (e.g., Romans 15:30, Colossians 4:2-4).

Action Plan and Strategies to Develop This Further:
- ✓ Make it a habit to offer words of encouragement to those around you, especially when they are facing challenges or doubts.
- ✓ Prioritize prayer both individually and as a community. Praying for each other's strength and faith can have a transformative effect.
- ✓ Create an atmosphere of openness within your community where individuals can share their struggles and doubts without fear of judgment.

The power of community is a cornerstone in the journey of rejecting grasshopper talk and embracing giant-killer faith. By fostering unity, accountability, encouragement, and prayer within your community, you not only strengthen your own faith but also empower others to reject defeatist mindsets and conquer their giants. Together, as a supportive community, you can achieve remarkable victories in faith and life.

Daily Action Plan to Avoid Grasshopper Talk and Focus on the Power of GOD to Overcome Giants

Avoiding "grasshopper talk" and focusing on the power of God in our lives to overcome giants is a daily practice that requires intention and commitment. Here's a daily action plan to help you cultivate this mindset:

Morning Routine:
1. **Morning Prayer and Meditation:** Start your day with prayer and meditation. Express gratitude for the day ahead and seek God's guidance and strength.
2. **Positive Affirmations:** Affirm your faith and belief in God's power. Repeat affirmations such as, "With God, I can overcome any giant" or "I trust in God's plan for my life." (See list of Declarations in the next chapter)
3. **Scripture Reading:** Read a relevant Bible verse that inspires faith and courage. For example, Psalm 18:32 says, *"It is God who arms me with strength and keeps my way secure."*

Throughout the Day:
1. **Mindfulness and Self-Awareness:** Be mindful of your thoughts and self-talk. When you catch yourself thinking negatively or doubting your abilities, pause and redirect your thoughts towards faith and trust in God.

2. **Gratitude Journal:** Keep a gratitude journal and jot down moments when you witness God's power or guidance in your life. This practice helps you focus on the positive and strengthens your faith.
3. **Prayer Breaks:** Take short breaks during the day to offer quick prayers or moments of gratitude. Pause to acknowledge God's presence in your daily activities.
4. **Encouraging Scripture Reminders:** Set up reminders on your phone or in your workspace with encouraging Bible verses. These serve as constant reminders of God's power and presence.

Evening Reflection:
1. **Daily Reflection:** Before bed, reflect on your day. Acknowledge moments when you resisted "grasshopper talk" and trusted in God's power. Celebrate your faith-filled actions.
2. **Evening Prayer:** End your day with a prayer of thanks and surrender/ yielding. Hand over your concerns and worries to God, trusting that He will guide you through challenges.

Weekly and Monthly Practices:
1. **Bible Study and Fellowship:** Engage in regular Bible study or attend a fellowship group where you can discuss and deepen your understanding of God's power and promises.
2. **Acts of Service:** Dedicate time each week to acts of service or volunteering. Serving others

reinforces your faith and reminds you of the impact of God's love.

3. **Personal Growth Reading:** Read books and materials that inspire personal growth and faith. Consider books by Christian authors or those that discuss overcoming challenges through faith.

Accountability and Support:

1. **Accountability Partner:** Partner with a trusted friend or mentor who can help hold you accountable for maintaining a positive mindset and avoiding "grasshopper talk."
2. **Prayer Requests:** Share your concerns and goals with your prayer community or church. The support of a praying community can provide strength and encouragement.

Remember that cultivating faith and avoiding "grasshopper talk" is a continuous process. It's normal to have moments of doubt or negativity, but with consistent effort and a reliance on God's power, you can develop a mindset that allows you to overcome giants in your life. Each day is an opportunity to strengthen your faith and trust in God's plan for your journey.

31 Declarations and Decrees to Speak Over to Avoid Grasshopper Talk and Focus on the Power of GOD to Overcome Giants

Here are 31 declarations and decrees based on Scripture that you can speak over your life to avoid "grasshopper talk" and focus on the power of God to overcome any giant. You can use one for each day of the month as a daily affirmation:

Day 1: Faith Declaration *Scripture: Mark 11:22* "I declare that I have unwavering faith in God, and with faith, I can move mountains."

Day 2: Courage Declaration *Scripture: Joshua 1:9* "I declare that I am strong and courageous, for God is with me wherever I go."

Day 3: Strength Declaration *Scripture: Philippians 4:13* "I declare that I can do all things through Christ who strengthens me."

Day 4: Victory Declaration *Scripture: 1 Corinthians 15:57* "I declare that I am victorious through Jesus Christ, and nothing can overcome me."

Day 5: Overcoming Fear *Scripture: 2 Timothy 1:7* "I declare that God has not given me a spirit of fear, but of power, love, and a sound mind."

Day 6: Peace Declaration *Scripture: Philippians 4:7* "I declare the peace of God that surpasses all understanding guards my heart and mind."

Day 7: Wisdom Declaration *Scripture: James 1:5* "I declare that I have wisdom from God, and I make wise decisions."

Day 8: Gratitude Declaration *Scripture: 1 Thessalonians 5:18* "I declare that I give thanks in all circumstances, for this is God's will for me."

Day 9: Hope Declaration *Scripture: Romans 15:13* "I declare that I abound in hope by the power of the Holy Spirit."

Day 10: Trust Declaration *Scripture: Proverbs 3:5-6* "I declare that I trust in the Lord with all my heart and lean not on my understanding."

Day 11: Resilience Declaration *Scripture: Romans 5:3-4* "I declare that I rejoice in suffering, for it produces perseverance and character."

Day 12: Purpose Declaration *Scripture: Jeremiah 29:11* "I declare that God has plans to prosper me, not to harm me, and to give me a future and a hope."

Day 13: Blessing Declaration *Scripture: Psalm 34:8* "I declare that I taste and see that the Lord is good, and I am blessed."

Day 14: Forgiveness Declaration *Scripture: Ephesians 4:32* "I declare that I am kind and compassionate, forgiving others as God forgave me."

Day 15: Authority Declaration *Scripture: Luke 10:19* "I declare that I have authority over all the power of the enemy, and nothing will harm me."

Day 16: Abundance Declaration *Scripture: Philippians 4:19* "I declare that my God will supply all my needs according to His riches in glory."

Day 17: Love Declaration *Scripture: 1 Corinthians 13:4-7* "I declare that I am patient, kind, and full of love, for love never fails."

Day 18: Healing Declaration *Scripture: Isaiah 53:5* "I declare that by His stripes, I am healed."

Day 19: Faithfulness Declaration *Scripture: 1 Corinthians 10:13* "I declare that God is faithful and will not let me be tempted beyond what I can bear."

Day 20: Abiding in God's Word *Scripture: Psalm 119:105* "I declare that God's Word is a lamp to my feet and a light to my path."

Day 21: God's Guidance *Scripture: Proverbs 16:9* "I declare that I commit my plans to the Lord, and He directs my steps."

Day 22: Trusting God's Timing *Scripture: Ecclesiastes 3:1* "I declare that there is a time for every purpose under heaven, and God's timing is perfect."

Day 23: Divine Protection *Scripture: Psalm 91:11-12* "I declare that God's angels watch over me, and I am safe in His shelter."

Day 24: Contentment Declaration *Scripture: Philippians 4:11* "I declare that I have learned to be content in all circumstances."

Day 25: Fruitfulness Declaration *Scripture: John 15:5* "I declare that I abide in Christ, and I bear much fruit."

Day 26: Purposeful Living *Scripture: Romans 8:28* "I declare that all things work together for good to those who love God and are called according to His purpose."

Day 27: Anointing Declaration *Scripture: 1 John 2:20* "I declare that I have an anointing from the Holy One, and I know all things."

Day 28: Proclaiming Victory *Scripture: 1 Corinthians 15:57* "I declare that I have victory through Jesus Christ, and I am more than a conqueror."

Day 29: Trusting God's Promises *Scripture: 2 Peter 1:4* "I declare that I am a partaker of God's divine nature and have His precious promises."

Day 30: Conqueror Declaration *Scripture: Romans 8:37* "I declare that I am a conqueror through Him who loves me."

Day 31: Faith-Filled Future *Scripture: Jeremiah 29:11* "I declare that God's plans for me include a hopeful and prosperous future."

Speak these declarations and decrees daily, believing in their truth and the power of God to help you overcome any giant in your life. Allow them to strengthen your faith, dispel doubts, and affirm your trust in God's unwavering support and guidance.

Conclusion

As you've already experienced, **'Rejecting Grasshopper Talk: From Grasshopper to Giant-Killer-*Defeating Giants Daily!*** is not just a book; it's a timeless guide to conquering the formidable giants that stand between you and your dreams. It's a journey that invites you to embrace a mindset filled with faith, courage, and unwavering determination. By weaving together the wisdom of biblical stories with contemporary examples and practical advice, this book empowers you to not just confront adversity but to rise above it and achieve your full potential.

Throughout these pages, you've encountered profound lessons that draw upon the timeless teachings of the Bible:

Lesson 1: The Grasshopper Mentality has shown you the origins of self-doubt and the psychology behind it. It has taught you that your perception of yourself can profoundly impact your growth and achievement.

Lesson 2: The Twelve Spies underscored the importance of diverse perspectives and teamwork in making sound decisions. You've learned that collective influence can shape your outlook on life's challenges.

Lesson 3: The Defeatist Report exposed the crippling effects of negativity and the power it holds to paralyze a community. It's a reminder to guard against the spread of defeatism.

Lesson 4: Joshua and Caleb: The Giant-Killers illuminated the significance of resilience, courage, and unwavering faith. You've seen that these qualities are essential for success in the face of adversity.

Lesson 5: Reframing Your Perspective unveiled the art of seeing challenges as opportunities. You've discovered techniques to shift from a grasshopper mentality to a giant-killer mindset.

Lesson 6: Overcoming Fear has empowered you to confront your fears head-on, realizing that courage is not the absence of fear but the willingness to act despite it.

Lesson 7: The Power of Faith has showcased the transformative power of unwavering belief, illustrating how faith can move mountains and lead to victorious outcomes.

Lesson 8: Taking Action has emphasized the importance of turning belief into tangible results through proactive steps and consistent effort.

Lesson 9: Navigating Setbacks has taught you to embrace setbacks as part of the journey, fostering resilience and perseverance to overcome challenges.

Lesson 10: Claiming Your Promised Land has shown you how to define your goals, develop a vision, and persevere on your path to achieving your dreams.

As you've journeyed through these pages, my hope is that you've discovered the giant-killer within you—a force of unwavering faith, resilience, and courage. May you boldly claim your own promised land, realizing your deepest desires and achieving remarkable victories in life.

Remember, this book is not the end; it's a beginning—a roadmap to guide you as you navigate the challenges and giants that lie ahead. As you continue on your path, draw strength from the lessons learned, and share your newfound wisdom with others who aspire to conquer their own giants. In doing so, you will not only transform your own life but also inspire and empower those around you to reject grasshopper talk and embrace a mindset of triumph and achievement.

May your journey be filled with faith, courage, and the resolute determination to conquer life's giants and claim your own promised land.

About the Author
'GERARD ASSEY'

Gerard Assey is a Graduate in Economics, a PGD in Management (HRD) and holds a Doctorate in Leadership. Gerard holds several International Qualifications in Sales, Debt Collection, Training & Teaching, and is a 'Fellow' of the prestigious 'Institute of Sales & Marketing Management'-UK, a Certified NLP Practitioner, a 'Certified Trainer', an 'Accredited Management Teacher-Behavioral Sciences', a 'Certified Competency Facilitator', a 'Certified Management Consultant'- (the International credentials of a professional management consultant, awarded in accordance with global standards of the ICMCI); and a Certification from the University of Michigan in 'Successful Negotiation: Essential Strategies and Skills'

He is also a Member of the 'National Association of Sales Professionals' backed with several years experience in varied industries, both in India and Overseas. He also holds an 'Etiquette Consultant' Certification from the USA (by Sue Fox, Author of Best Seller: 'Business Etiquette for Dummies'. She has trained some of the top celebrities' world over). He was also a recipient of a scholarship for extensive training in Japan on 'Corporate Management for India'.

Gerard Assey is 'Founder & Chief Corporate Trainer' of the Group: **'Citius, Altius, Fortius Unlimited'**- an organization that **celebrated 20 years of Glorious Service** in 2021, focusing on 3 Core Competencies:

People. Performance. Profit; in functional areas of Sales & Marketing, HR & Organizational Development, covering Recruitment, Training & Consultancy!

Having managed organizations with large Sales Forces in India & Overseas, his specialization cover extensive areas of Sales Training (All levels - Presentation, Negotiation, Key/ Strategic Accounts Management & Managerial Skills for all sectors), Bid Proposal/ Capture Planning/ Management Trainings, Retail Sales, Customer Service & Customer Retention Programs, Training for Prevention & Collection of Debt, Self & Personal Development Programs (Time Management, Teamwork & Team Building, Business Etiquette & Personal Grooming, Leadership & Managerial Skills, People Management Skills, Train-the-Trainer etc), including preparation of Custom-designed Business Manuals for Internal (HR, Induction, and Sales etc) & External use (Instruction, User Manuals).

Gerard has successfully conducted over 6000 Trainings & Workshops (as of Oct '23) all across India, Middle East, Africa, Europe & S.E. Asia. Besides public programs conducted regularly, both in India & Overseas, he has some of the top names as clients whom he services from Single Owners to large Public & Government undertakings, covering all sectors, for their in-house needs.

His website: www.CollectionSkills.com is the only one in this part of the world to be featured in the 'Collections & Credit Risk Magazine-USA' under 'Who's Who in Training' and ranks TOP, along with other websites listed below on most search engines.

Gerard is author of 79 books already (Oct 2023),

A Few of the Business related Books being:

1. Bite-sized Bits on Commonsense Management
2. Heart to Heart on Life's Principles'
3. How to become a Successful Manager
4. The Sales Professionals' Master Workbook of S.Y.S.T.E.M.S
5. The Professional Business Email Etiquette Handbook & Guide
6. The Professional Business Video-Conferencing Etiquette Handbook & Guide
7. Professional Presentation Skills
8. Exceptional Customer Service
9. Professional Tele-Marketing Skills
10. Professional Debt Collection Skills
11. The G.R.E.A.T. Sales & Service Workbook
12. Sales Training Advantage for Results (*The Ultimate Sales Training Manual to enable you stand out as a S.T.A.R.*)
13. CEO Daily Planner & Organizer
14. The Sales Professionals' Master Daily Planner
15. The Professional Debt Collector's Master Daily Planner
16. My Daily Planner & Organizer
17. MY EMERGENCY INFORMATION RECORD (Family Emergency & Peace of Mind Planner)
18. The Ultimate Therapist & Counselors Planner and Organizer
19. Building an Ethical Workplace
20. Managing Relationships at Work
21. Managing Business Meetings Effectively
22. Effective Delegation Skills
23. Goal Setting for Success
24. B2B Selling by Email
25. Professional Business Etiquette & Grooming
26. Dining Etiquette & Table Manners
27. Effective Networking Skills
28. Grooming, Etiquette & Manners for Teens, Young Adults & Future Leaders
29. Inter-Personal Skills

...And some of his most recent Christian Books being:

1. A Bouquet of Praises for My KING
2. Christian Jokes for the Serious Religious' Folks!
3. Jesus Healed You!
4. Praise24Ever! (also in Tamil version)
5. The 5G Network of GOD
6. Building Faith over F.E.A.R- FACE EVERYTHING AND RISE with JESUS
7. Hebrew and Greek Praise and Worship Words
8. Godly Mothers' and Grandmothers' Bible Story time for Kids!
9. Miracles of Jesus in Pictures
10. Raise your Praise all 365 Days
11. Thanking GOD with an Attitude of Gratitude
12. Meditating on the Attributes of GOD
13. Puppet Scripts
14. Alcohol Ruins, JESUS Reforms, Renews & Restores!
15. Habakkuk 2:2 Christian Daily Journal, Planner & Organizer
16. ABC of GOD's Word for Handwriting Practice
17. Daily Bible Verse Handwriting Practice (Building Godly Character & Faith through Cursive Handwriting Practice!)
18. Guiding Light: Fun & Faith-Building Bible Activities for Children

Besides regularly contributing to business & trade journals, including international ones such as the 'Creative Training Techniques' and the 'Sales News' of the U.S.A, He is also a member of several prestigious bodies & trade associations, having participated in many Conferences & Workshops in India & Overseas.

Prior to his last assignment of leading & managing a large MNC as head, Gerard had a 3-year stint in the

Middle East as a Consultant with a leading British Consultancy Firm.

As the past 'Official Country Representative' for the International Business Award- 'THE STEVIES'-(the business world's own Oscar) for about 4 years- he ensured a few Indian companies that qualify for the same every year!

Gerard can be contacted at:
Email: training@Sales-Training.in,training@CollectionSkills.com
Websites:

      www.Sales-Training.in
      www.EtiquetteWorks.in
      www.CollectionSkills.com
      www.RetailSalesTraining.in
      www.SalesTrainingIndia.com
      www.ManualPreparation.com
      www.TrainingWithPuppets.com
      www.FirstContactAcademy.com
      www.SalesAndMarketingRecruiter.com

Our **TRAININGS & BOOKS** that can help your team

- ✓ **Sales Effectiveness**: Selling Skills for any Sector: Service/ Logistics/ FMCG Realty/ Insurance & Finance/ Media/ SPA's, Health Clubs & Salons/ Key Account Management, Effective Negotiation Skills/ Bid & Proposal Management Skills/ Retail Sales Training: Any Sector (Auto, Jewelry, Clothing, Luxury etc)
- ✓ **Customer Service Skills**-Complaints Handling & Customer Retention
- ✓ **Debt Prevention & Collection Skills**
- ✓ **Etiquette & Grooming**
- ✓ **Leadership & Managerial Skills**
- ✓ **Self & Personal Development Skills**: Presentation Skills/ Effective Communication Skills/Business Proposal Writing Skills/ Problem Solving & Decision Making Skills/ Empowering Secretaries-The perfect PA! (For Secretaries & PA's)/ Effective Time Management/ Teamwork & Teambuilding/ P.R.I.D.E- **P**ersonal **R**esponsibility **I**n **D**elivering Excellence